STUDY GUIDE

HOW TO HOLD YOUR PASTOR'S LADDER

Published by AVAIL

Cover design by: Joe De Leon of DeLeon Designs
Cover photo by: Andrew van Tilborgh

ISBN: 978-1-969062-10-0 1 2 3 4 5 6 7 8 9 10

Printed in the United States of America

STUDY GUIDE

HOW TO HOLD YOUR PASTOR'S LADDER

SAM CHAND

CONTENTS

HOW
TO HOLD
YOUR
PASTOR'S
LADDER
SAM
CHAND

CHAPTER 1

THE LADDER STORY

Ladder holders aren't a suggestion or option—they are vital for pastors.

READING TIME

As you read Chapter 1: "The Ladder Story" in *How to Hold Your Pastor's Ladder*, reflect on, and respond to the text by answering the following questions.

REFLECT AND TAKE ACTION:

What comes to mind when you think about being a ladder holder for your pastor?

"Those who hold the ladder control the ascent of the pastor." How have your words, expectations, or actions affected your pastor's ability to climb higher—or made that climb more difficult?

When you consider the pastor's many responsibilities—spiritual, emotional, and administrative—where do you most clearly see opportunities for you or your team to share the weight instead of adding to it?

What "small" tasks have you dismissed in your church that might actually be vital for your pastor's security or encouragement?

What motives drive your involvement in ministry, and how can you purify them so that service remains selfless?

Previous ladder holders may not be able to hold new ladders as vision expands. In what ways might you or your church need to grow, retrain, or release old habits to support a new level of vision?

What meaningful questions could you ask your pastor this week to better understand how to support them—spiritually, emotionally, or practically—in their climb?

CHAPTER 2

PASTORS SEE IT ALL!

Let's be honest: some people who claim to support their pastor do more harm than good.

READING TIME

As you read Chapter 2: "Pastors See It All!" in *How to Hold Your Pastor's Ladder*, reflect on, and respond to the text by answering the following questions.

REFLECT AND TAKE ACTION:

When you picture your pastor's week, what unseen burdens do you think they carry that you may have never acknowledged before?

Many people expect their pastor to "be available 24/7" while rarely considering how much they give. In what ways might you have unintentionally added to your pastor's weight—and what could you change to ease that burden?

Reflect on the comparison between the "faithful ladder holder" and the "ladder shaker." Which behaviors—criticism, inconsistency, distraction, or genuine care—do you most see in yourself, and what steps could help you become a steadier support?

There are several dysfunctional ladder holders: casual, distracted, and shaking. Which of these tendencies most threatens the culture of your church, and what could you personally do to help correct it?

What are some simple, intentional actions you could take to remind your pastor they are not alone—especially in emotionally heavy or discouraging seasons?

Many people limit pastor appreciation to one weekend a year. What consistent rhythms of encouragement could you personally adopt to make pastoral support part of your lifestyle rather than a seasonal gesture?

When was the last time you expressed gratitude to your pastor or their family without a specific occasion? How might practicing spontaneous encouragement—"just because"—reshape your relationship with your leaders?

CHAPTER 3

NINE THINGS PASTORS WISH THEIR CHURCHES KNEW ABOUT THEM

The church doesn't just need more attendees; it needs people willing to take ownership of the mission.

READING TIME

As you read Chapter 3: "Nine Things Pastors Wish Their Churches Knew About Them" in *How to Hold Your Pastor's Ladder*, reflect on, and respond to the text by answering the following questions.

REFLECT AND TAKE ACTION:

Which of the nine things pastors wish their churches knew surprised you the most—or stood out to you most—as it relates to your own pastor? Why?

How do you personally respond when a message doesn't resonate as deeply as you hoped? What would it look like to extend grace rather than criticism?

How aware are you of the ways ministry affects your pastor's spouse and children, and what specific gesture could you make to help restore joy or normalcy to their family life?

Reflect on the practical boundaries listed—respecting family time, personal time, and days off. Which of these boundaries do you think your pastor struggles most to protect, and what could you do to help honor that margin rather than encroach on it?

How might outdated thinking about pastoral compensation reveal hidden attitudes toward money, ministry, or worth in your church culture?

If you were to start a rhythm of prayer for your pastor this week, what would that practically look like—daily, weekly, or corporately? Who could you invite to join you?

Where have you drifted into consuming rather than contributing, and what area of service could you step into that would lighten your pastor's load and strengthen the mission?

CHAPTER 4

INSIDE THE MIND OF A PASTOR

Everyone expects something of them.
Few truly understand the cost.

READING TIME

As you read Chapter 4: "Inside the Mind of a Pastor" in *How to Hold Your Pastor's Ladder*, reflect on, and respond to the text by answering the following questions.

REFLECT AND TAKE ACTION:

When you think about your pastor's week, what moments do you imagine might be hardest for them to truly rest—and what could you do to help create space for their rest?

When was the last time you truly noticed signs of mental or emotional fatigue in your pastor—or did you assume they were fine? What does that assumption reveal about how you see spiritual leadership?

Reflect on this question: "Would you work in a place where people voted on you every week by their attendance, giving, and participation?" If your pastor's sense of progress were measured by your consistency, what story would the data tell?

What expectations do you personally place on your pastor—spoken or unspoken—and which of them might need to change?

Many pastors struggle with action bias—feeling they must constantly be producing results. How might your church culture (or your own impatience) reinforce that pressure? Where could you practice patience instead of demanding visible progress?

Pastors are often criticized for being "too passive" by some and "too assertive" by others. Think of a moment when you disagreed with your pastor's leadership style. What emotion—fear, pride, control, disappointment—was really beneath your reaction?

Pastors are constantly adjusting—structurally, financially, and relationally—while longing for stability. How well do you handle change in your church? When transitions occur, are you a source of peace or of passive resistance?

CHAPTER 5

SHIFTS IN A PASTOR'S JOURNEY

The weight of pastoring is not about how much pastors carry, but how wisely they choose what to carry.

READING TIME

As you read Chapter 5: "Shifts in a Pastor's Journey" in *How to Hold Your Pastor's Ladder*, reflect on, and respond to the text by answering the following questions.

REFLECT AND TAKE ACTION:

When you look at your church culture, which do you think your congregation fears more—change or stagnation—and what does that fear reveal about your collective mindset?

Pastors often wrestle between expanding vision and personal limitation—wanting to "cut back and move forward at the same time." When have you personally experienced that same tension in your own calling or career, and how does that help you relate to your pastor's journey?

How do you respond when your pastor begins to bring in new people or ideas that challenge the way things have always been done? Do you see it as disloyalty—or as leadership maturity? Explain.

When your church enters uncertain or uncomfortable territory, what is your natural instinct: to anchor, to adapt, or to abandon ship?

What would it take for you to create an environment where your pastor feels free to learn, experiment, or even fail without judgment?

Shift #6 reminds us that "old flames may dim, but new ones can ignite." Have you noticed areas where your pastor's passion seems to be shifting? What emotions—hope, fear, or skepticism—does that stir in you, and why?

When your pastor pursues something that feels risky or fast-moving, do you instinctively cheer them on or slow them down? What might that reveal about your comfort with risk and trust in leadership?

CHAPTER 6

PASTORAL PAINS

Pastors are the CEOs of their churches, so they're never off.

READING TIME

As you read Chapter 6: "Pastoral Pains" in *How to Hold Your Pastor's Ladder*, reflect on, and respond to the text by answering the following questions.

REFLECT AND TAKE ACTION:

"Every advancement introduces a new ache." What does that reveal about your own assumptions regarding growth in ministry—do you subconsciously expect expansion without suffering?

The text compares leadership pain to childbirth, where vision gives meaning to pressure. When have you experienced a form of "productive pain" that produced something worthwhile? How does that reframe the way you view your pastor's endurance?

Where have you seen church members value control over connection, and what effect has that had on unity or trust in leadership?

Think of a moment when outside forces—a law, economy, cultural debate—affected your church's direction. How did you interpret your pastor's response then, and what do you see differently now?

Why do you think it's difficult for congregations to imagine their pastor as insecure, and how might that assumption distort expectations?

If every visible success in your church came with invisible scars on your pastor's soul, how would it change the way you measure "fruitfulness"?

When your church grows busier or more complicated, where do you personally feel tempted to withdraw, complain, or oversimplify? What would maturity look like instead?

CHAPTER 7

FIVE TRAITS OF GREAT LADDER HOLDERS

If your grip shifts with every conversation, you were never holding the ladder—just brushing against it.

READING TIME

As you read Chapter 7: "Five Traits of Great Ladder Holders" in *How to Hold Your Pastor's Ladder*, reflect on, and respond to the text by answering the following questions.

REFLECT AND TAKE ACTION:

When you think about your church culture, where might the "base" feel unstable—not because of programs, but because of people's posture?

When life or ministry gets heavy, do you tend to absorb pressure, transfer it, or create more of it? What does that reveal about your inner strength?

When was the last time you faced correction or challenge in ministry? Did it make you defensive or adaptive—and what would growth look like in that same moment now?

How do you personally react when your pastor or leader sees something differently than you do? What might that moment expose about the condition of your heart?

When are you most tempted to mentally check out of what God's doing—and how does that affect those counting on you?

What does faithfulness cost you personally—time, comfort, anonymity, ego—and why is that cost worth paying?

If your church's culture were sensed only by your attitude, reliability, and speech, what would it taste like—strong and steady, or bitter and unstable? Explain.

Looking back over everything you've read in this study, what truth has stayed with you the most, and what specific change will you make in how you relate to your pastor or serve your church?

www.ingramcontent.com/pod-product-compliance
Lightning Source LLC
LaVergne TN
LVHW010842120826
845149LV00020B/3489
* 9 7 8 1 9 6 9 0 6 2 1 0 0 *